Contents

2	Introduction/The Romans
4	Canterbury 30 CE
6	Canterbury 60 CE
8	Canterbury 150 CE
10	Canterbury 300 CE
12	The Roman Theatre
14	The Basilica and Forum
16	The Temple Precinct
18	The Public Bathhouse
20	The Townhouse
22	The Roman Town Wall
24	Ridingate
26	The Roman Army
28	The Roman Pottery Kilns
30	The Pudding Pan Pots
32	Roman Canterbury today

Symbols used in this guide

1 *Roman site, with visible remains*

2 *Roman site, with no visible remains*

3 *Speculative location of Roman site*
(Other Roman towns of Canterbury's importance had these sites, but no evidence of them has yet been found)

— *Roman wall, no visible remains*

A *The Canterbury Roman Museum*

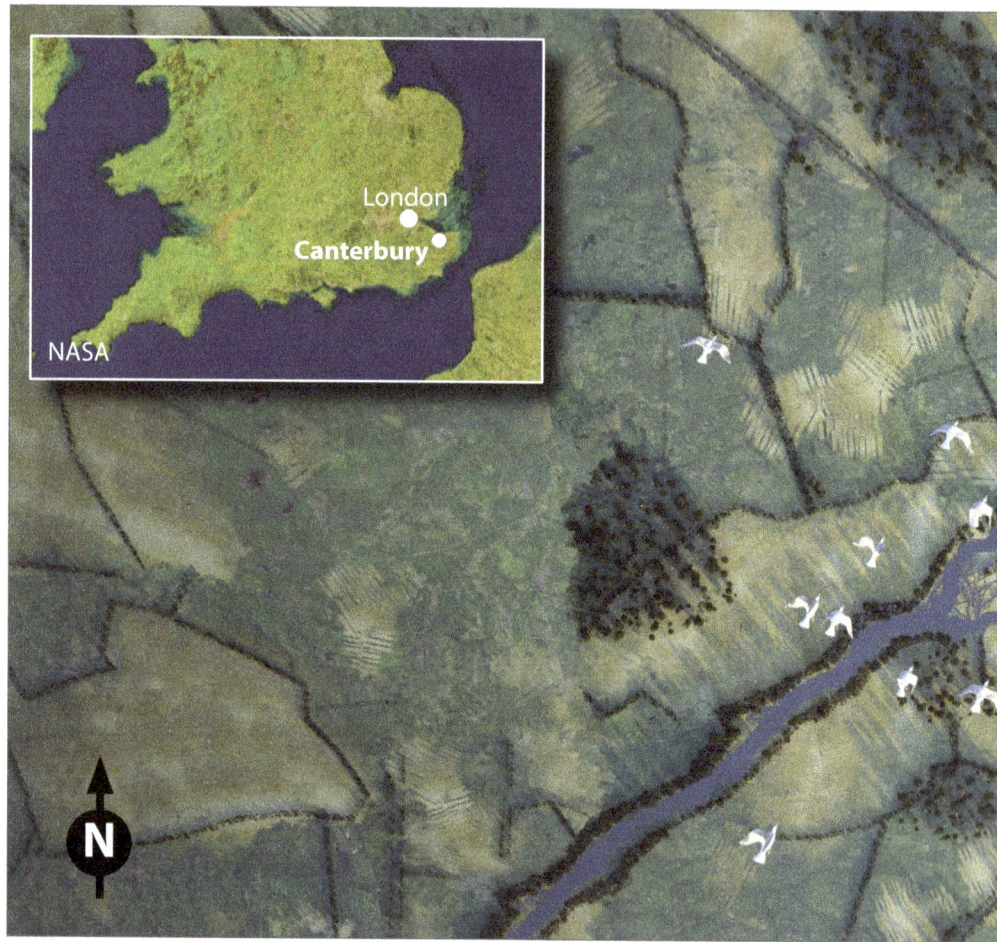

Canterbury, looking north, 300 CE.

Introduction

Canterbury has a long and complex history, spanning over two thousand years. This guide explores how Canterbury evolved from 30 CE to 300 CE. In this time it changed from a capital of the *Cantiaci* tribe to a bustling commercial hub connected to major Roman seaports. After this date the Roman Empire started a gradual decline and by 410 CE Britain was under constant attack by marauding Anglo-Saxons. The guide features full-colour reconstructions all looking north *(unless specified otherwise)*, showing key points in Roman Canterbury's history and important sites, such as the Roman theatre and townhouse. Modern maps allow you to compare the past with present day Canterbury.

Towns and cities
The Romans defined towns and cities differently to how we do in the present day. They had three main types of town:
- *A Colonia, which was a rough equivalent of a city.*
- *A Municipium, which was slightly less important than a colonia.*
- *A Civitas capital, which was a broad equivalent of a large market town.*

The Romans called pre-Roman towns 'oppida'.

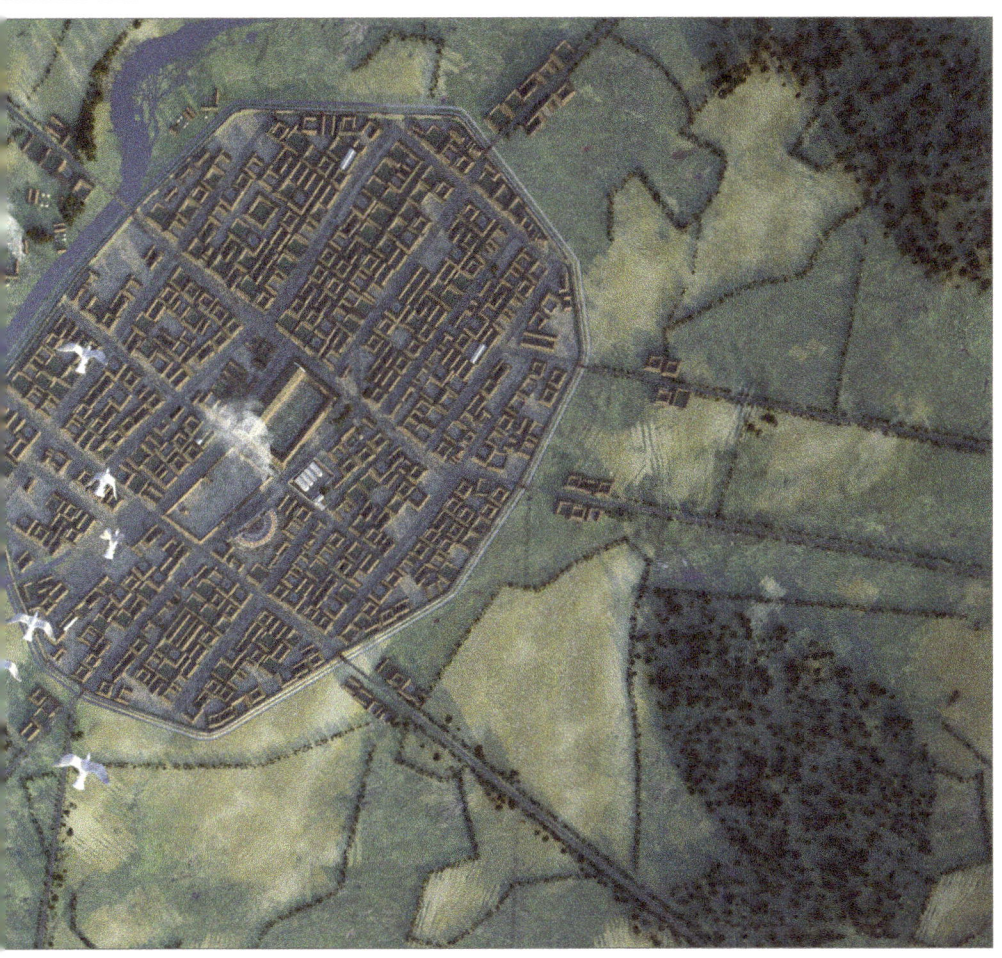

The Romans

The city of Rome in central Italy was formed around 800 BCE and grew over the centuries into the Roman Empire, which covered most of Europe, the Middle East and North Africa. It was a highly sophisticated and technologically advanced society, with a huge army, major roads and large cities. Britain at that time was a mysterious place with fierce tribes and valuable metals, which became the focus of two attempted invasions in 55 BCE and 54 BCE by *Julius Caesar*. Those invasions were repelled by local tribes and the Romans did not try again to invade Britain for almost 100 years. By 43 CE the *Emperor Claudius (who needed the army's support)* decided to invade Britain, which was weakened by the death of *King Cunobelin* of the *Trinovantes*, who lived in *Camulodunum (Colchester)*. After attacking Colchester the Emperor's forces then moved across England including where present day Canterbury is located...

Visiting Canterbury
Canterbury lies about 62 miles (100 km) south-east of London. The Canterbury Roman Museum has mosaics, artefacts and more, found in and around Canterbury. Most Roman sites mentioned in this book are no longer visible, apart from a couple of sections of the Roman Wall.

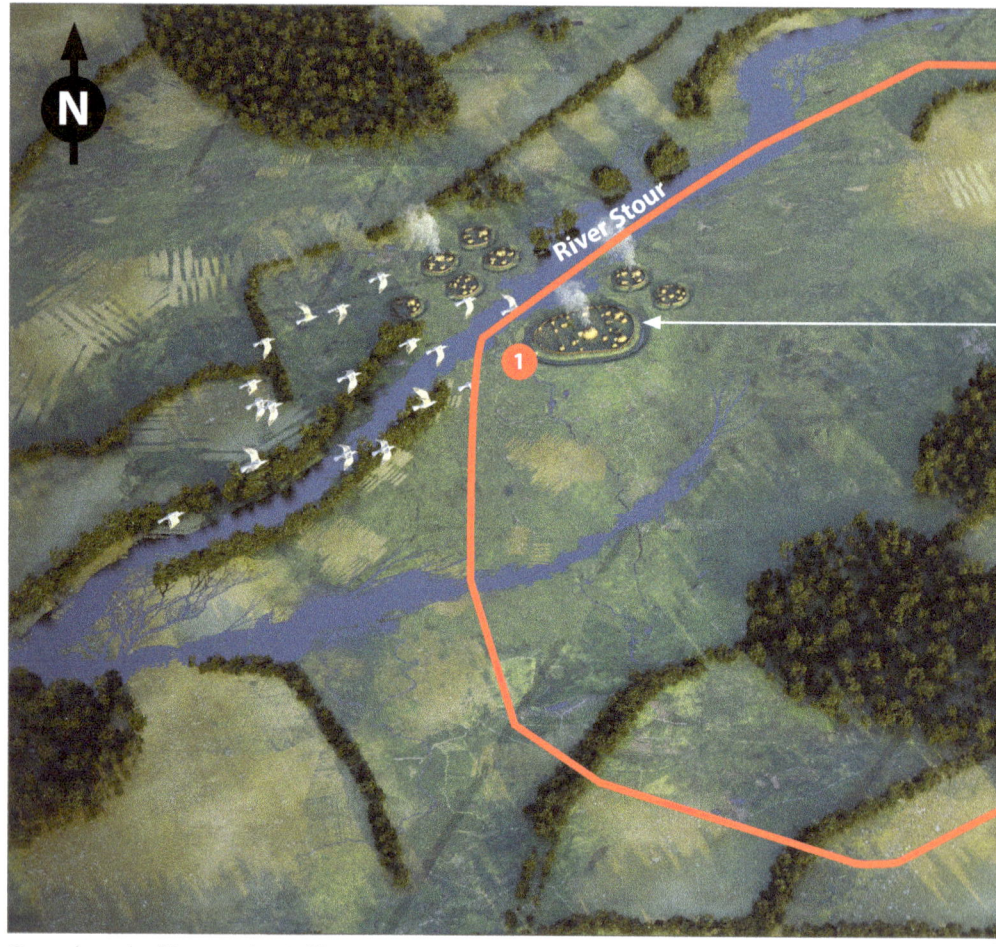

Canterbury, looking north, 30 CE

Canterbury 30 CE

The area where Canterbury is located had long been occupied before the Roman invasion and had strong ties with continental Europe. Around 150 BCE *Belgic*[1] tribes occupied the lands of local British tribes in the south, then started to form into distinct new tribes which occupied areas that roughly match where the present day counties are. One of these tribes was known by the Romans as the '*Cantiaci*', whose territory was centred in Bigbury hillfort about 3 miles *(5 km)* west of present day Canterbury in Kent. Some of the Cantiaci moved to the Canterbury area, calling it *Durovernon*.[2]

1. Pre-Roman tribes who lived in the Belgium, France and Luxembourg area.
2. This is thought to mean the 'Fort by the alder grove'.

Key

— *Future Roman Town Wall*
① *Durovernon*
② *Cantiaci Roundhouse*

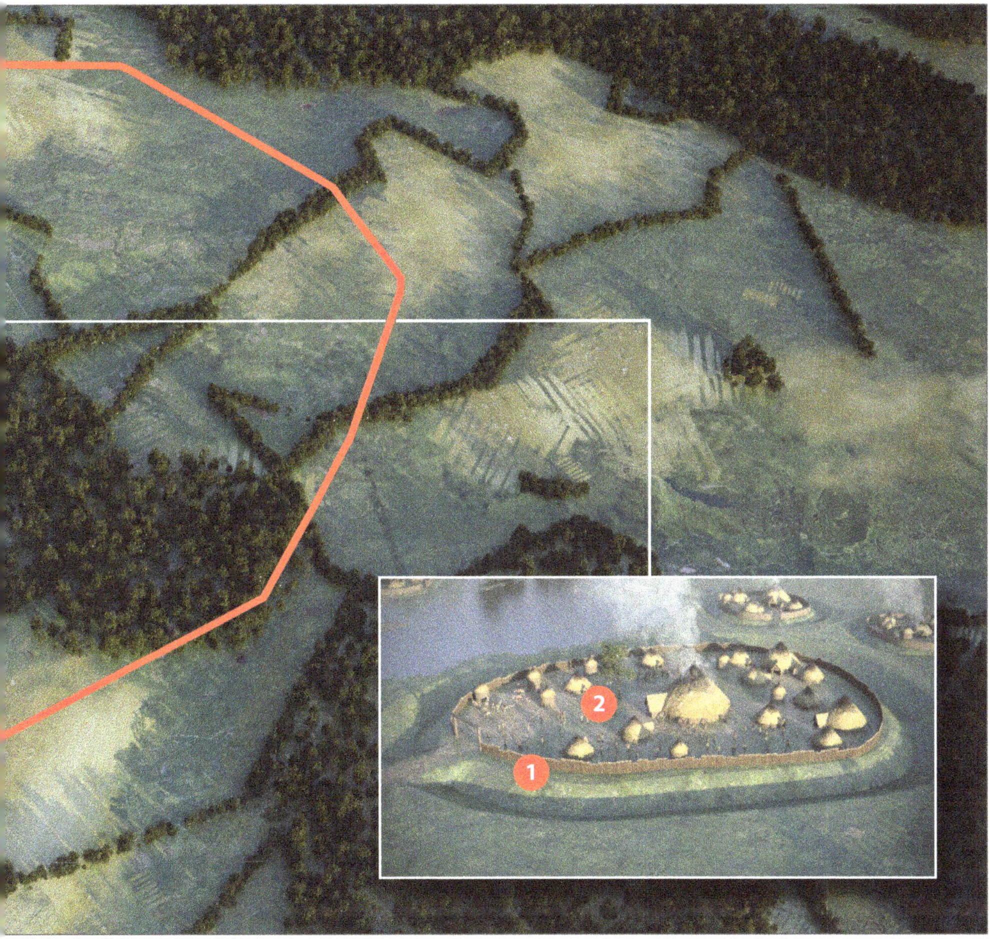

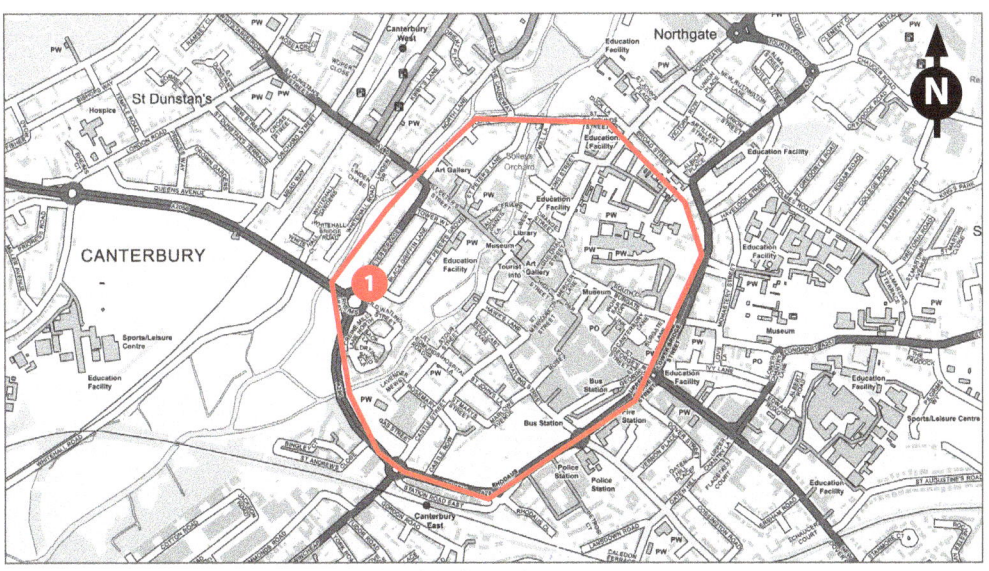

Contains Ordnance Survey data © Crown copyright and database right 2025

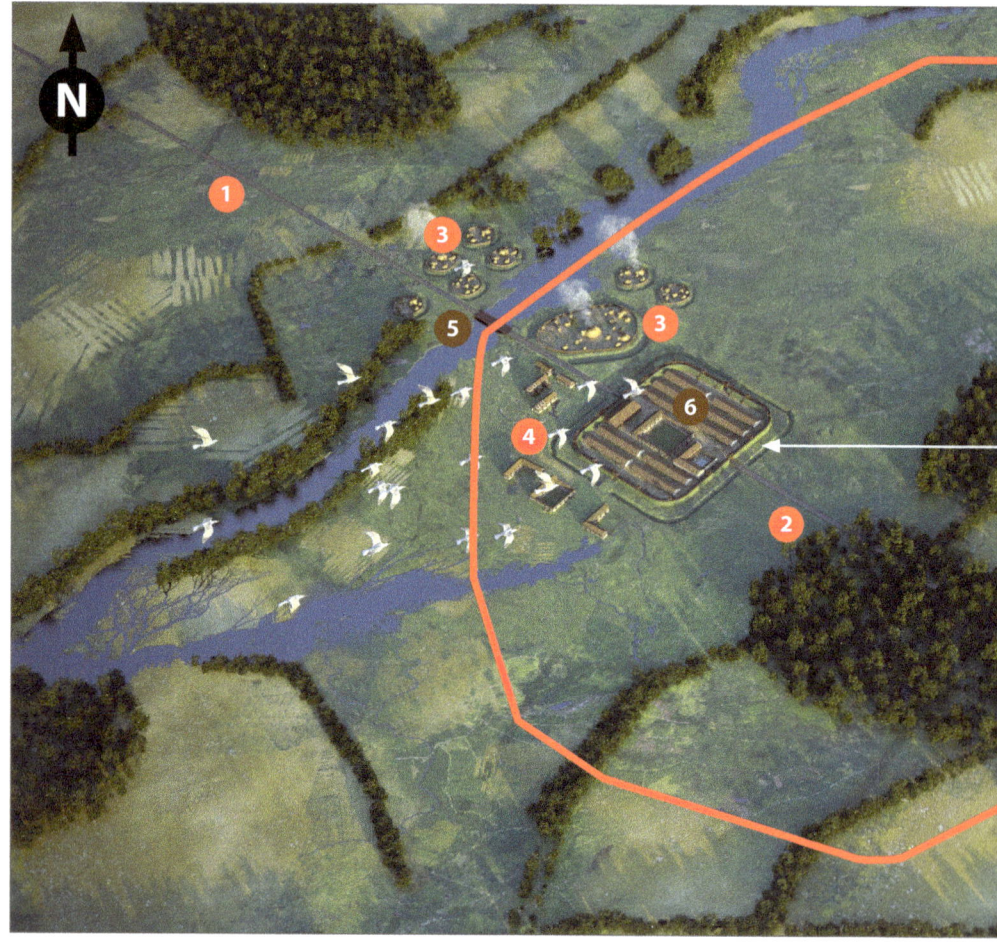

Canterbury, looking north, 60 CE.

Canterbury 60 CE

After the invasion of 43 CE, the legions started to move out across Britain. As they did this they built roads, fortresses and supply bases. The area where *Durovernon (Canterbury)* is now lay at a strategic crossing of the River Stour, where roads from newly established Roman ports converged at Canterbury. These ports included: *Rutupiae (Richborough), Dubris (Dover)* and *Portus Lemanis (Lympne)*. A Roman presence was established in 43 CE, but the main military base in the area was at *Rutupiae*. *Durovernon* slowly grew, due to its location with passing soldiers and traders.

In 60-61 CE nearby London was destroyed by *Boudica* and 120,000 warriors. But luckily for *Durovernon* she and her forces moved north instead of south, towards St. Albans. For around the next 40 years the town was a collection of Roman style houses and *Cantiaci* roundhouses, although part of the town was subject to occasional flooding.

Key

— *Future Roman Town Wall*
1. *Road to London*
2. *Road to Dover*
3. *Cantiaci roundhouse*
4. *Trading settlement*
5. *Bridge or ferry*
6. *Fort*[1]

1. It is believed that some kind of fort was built in Canterbury, due to its strategic location. No evidence of one has yet been found, so this **highly speculative** view is based on a fort found in Dover.

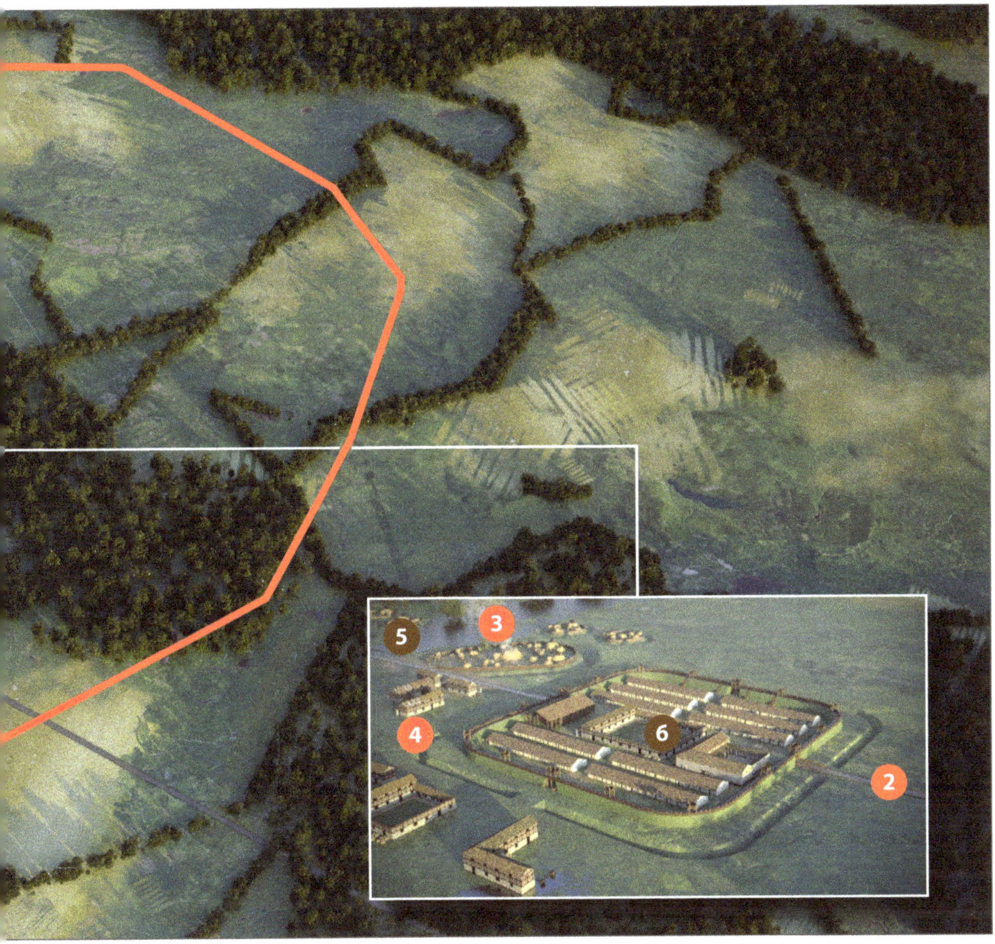

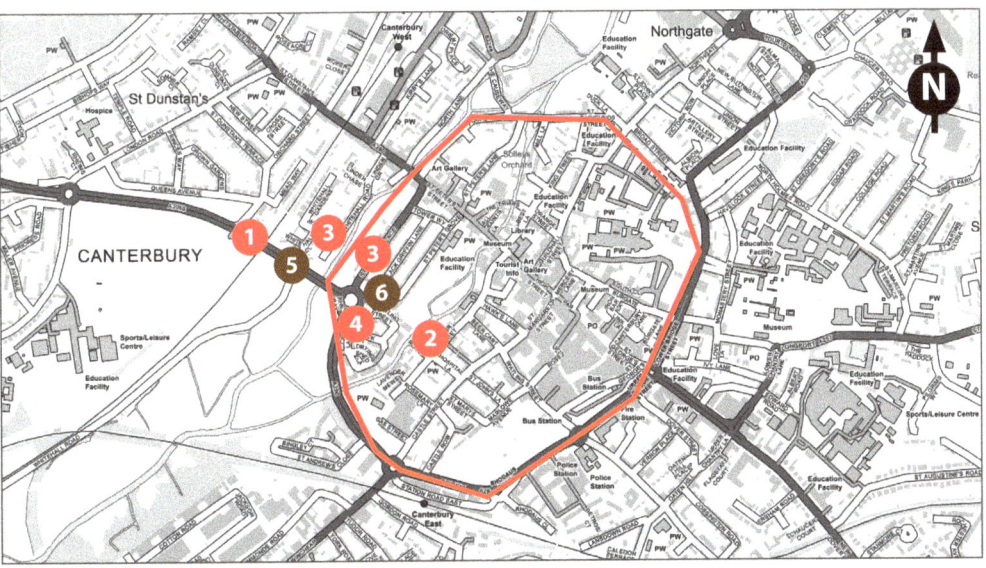

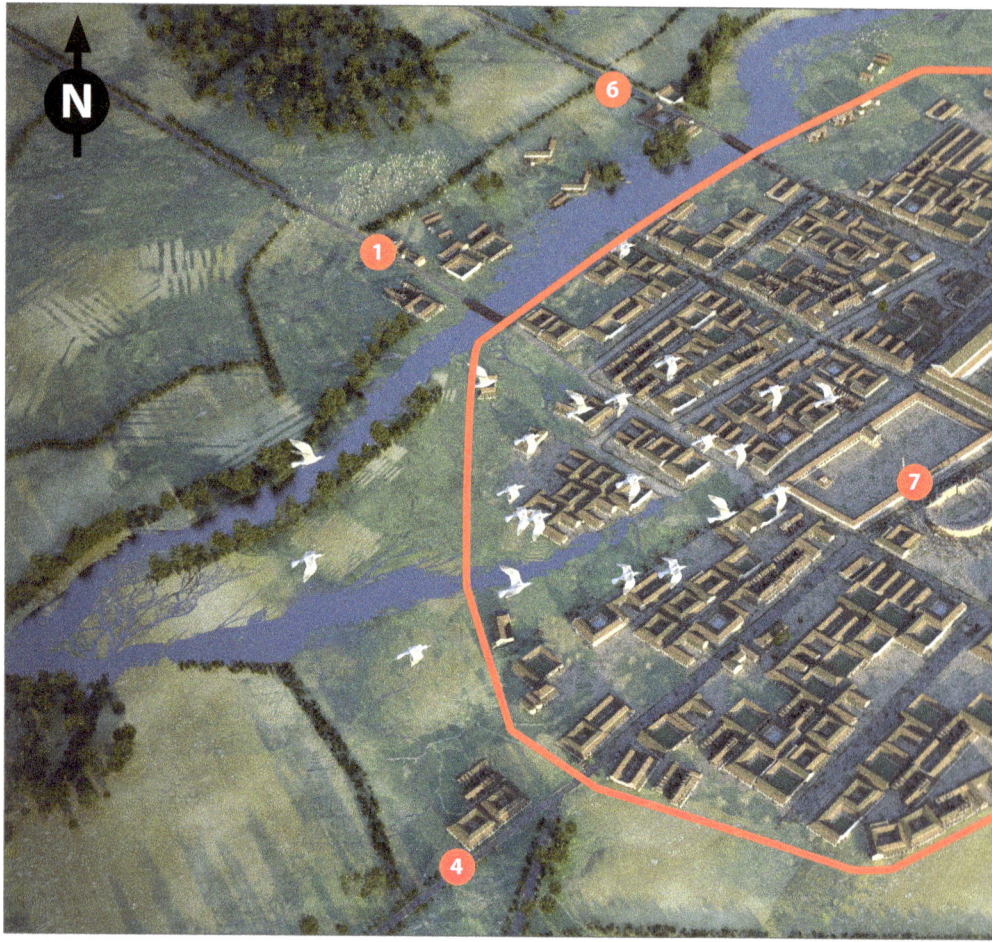

Canterbury, looking north, 150 CE.

Canterbury 150 CE

Around 110 CE *Durovernon (Canterbury)* started to have a large amount of public buildings constructed, including: a theatre, a basilica/forum, temples and a public bathhouse.[1] The town now had the typical Roman grid system of streets connecting to the network of roads which converged on *Durovernon*. One of these roads was Watling Street, parts of which still exist in the present day, connecting the seaports to London *(via Canterbury)*, St Albans and right across to Wroxeter, which lies near to the North Wales border. Around 190 CE *Durovernon* had become a *civitas*,[2] known as *Durovernum Cantiacorum*.[3] Some of the private houses were upgraded with stone construction, underfloor heating and fine mosaics.

1. These are shown later in this book.
2. A Civitas was a broad equivalent of a large market town.
3. Meaning loosely 'Fort of the Cantiaci by the alder grove'.

Key

— Future Roman Town Wall
1. Watling Street to London
2. Watling Street to Dover
3. Road to Richborough
4. Road to Lympne
5. Road to Reculver
6. Road towards Whitstable
7. The original version of the Roman Theatre, which was upgraded around 220 CE.

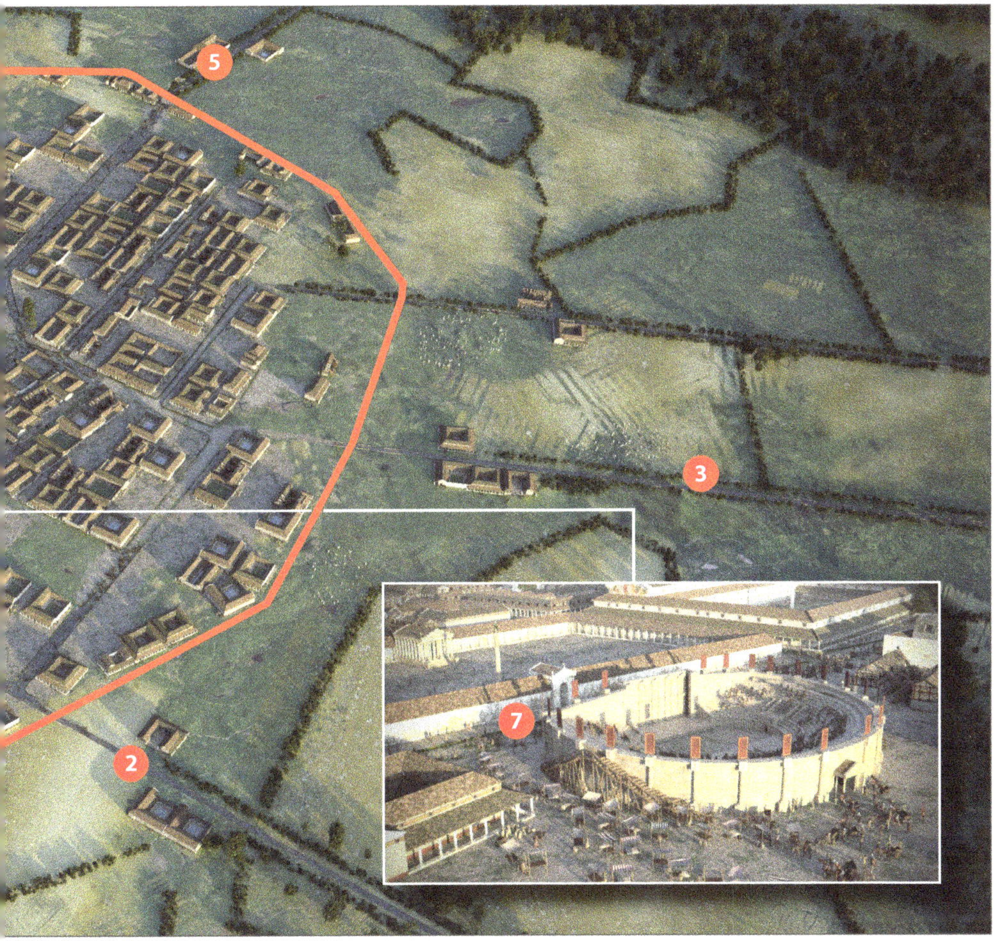

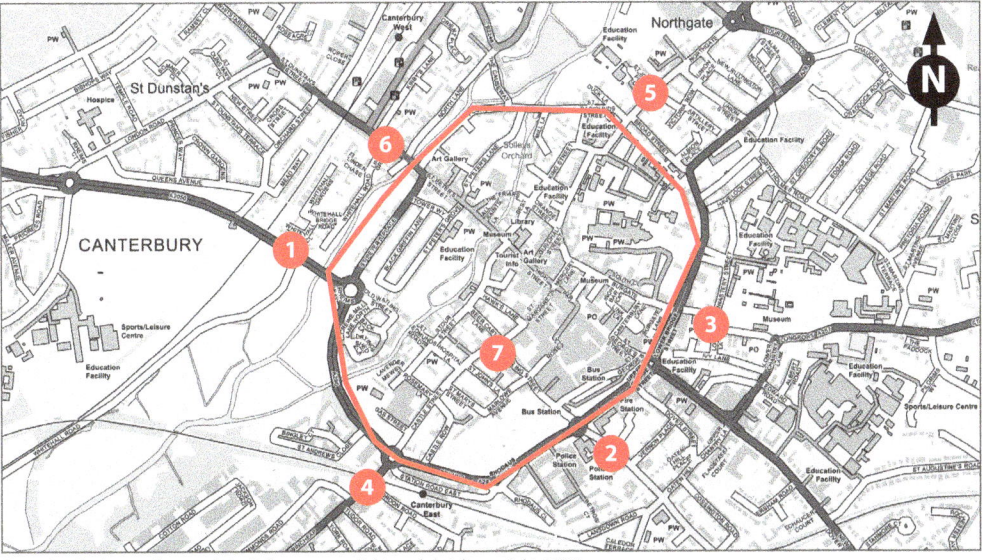

10. Canterbury 300 CE

Canterbury, looking north, 300 CE.

Canterbury 300 CE

Roman Britain and the wider Roman Empire were slowly starting to fall to pieces. In addition, external forces were starting to attack the edges of the empire. This led to many Roman towns in Britain improving their defences. Canterbury was no exception, and by this time a huge wall with gatehouses surrounded the town. Most of these gatehouses would have had a single archway, except for those which joined Watling Street. These gatehouses would have had double arches, one at London Gate and one at Ridingate. But in just over 100 years Canterbury and most other Roman towns were abandoned, as the Roman empire fell. Around 200 years later a small Anglo-Saxon settlement was living amongst the ruins. *"...the work of giants is decaying..."* part of a poem written in Anglo-Saxon times, gives a sense of the Anglo-Saxons' unease and wonder about who built the towns they now occupied.

Key

— Roman Town Wall
1. London Gate
2. Ridingate
3. Gatehouse
4. Theatre
5. Basilica/Forum
6. Temple Precinct
7. Bathhouse
8. Cemetery
9. Kiln
10. Townhouse
11. Town Wall
12. Queningate

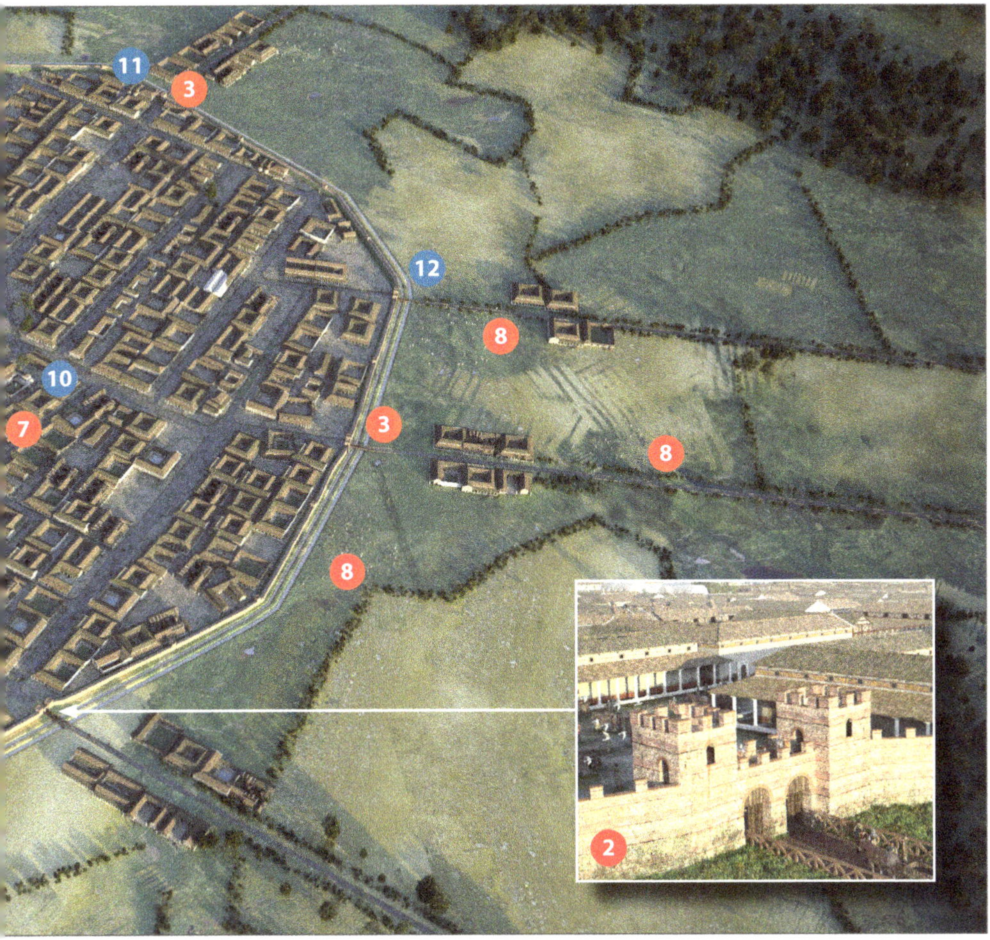

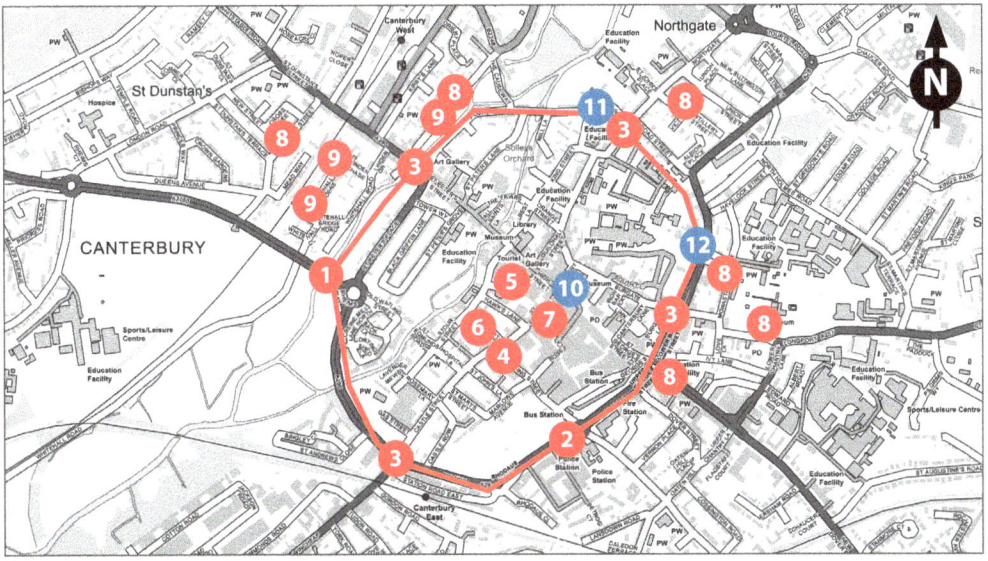

12. *The Roman Theatre*

The Roman Theatre, looking north, 300 CE.

The Roman Theatre

Canterbury, as with many other Roman towns, had a theatre. Pantomimes were more popular than plays, as well as comedies based on people's lives. This theatre may have also had religious events, as it was near to a temple. It was built around 100 CE[1] and had wooden outer stairs and wooden internal seating. Eventually it seated about 3000 people when it was upgraded around 220 CE. The building may have stood over 16 metres *(52 feet)* tall with a large and complex stage area including the *Scaenae frons*, which was full of columns and provided a background for the actors. The audience would have entered the theatre through the *Vomitorium* and sat in the semi-circular *Auditorium*, overlooking the *Orchestra (stage)*. It is thought that the theatre survived until around the time of the Norman Conquest, almost 1,000 years later.

1. See page 8.

Key

— Roman Theatre Wall
1. Roman Theatre
2. Basilica/Forum
3. Temple Precinct
4. Bathhouse
5. Triumphal Arch
6. Scaenae Frons
7. Vomitorium
8. Auditorium

N
2
8
6
4
1
7

N
Museum
HIGH STREET
MERCERY LANE
2
HAWK'S LANE
ST MARGARET'S STREET
4
PO
OLD WATLING STREET
BACK LA
BEER CART LANE
3
STOUR STREET
ST EDMUNDS ROAD
HOSPITAL LA
1
5
WATLING STREET
ROSE LA
PW
LAVENDER MEWS
Bus Station
ROSEMARY LA
ST JOHN'S LA
ST MARYS STREET
MARLOWE AVENUE
Bus Station
PW

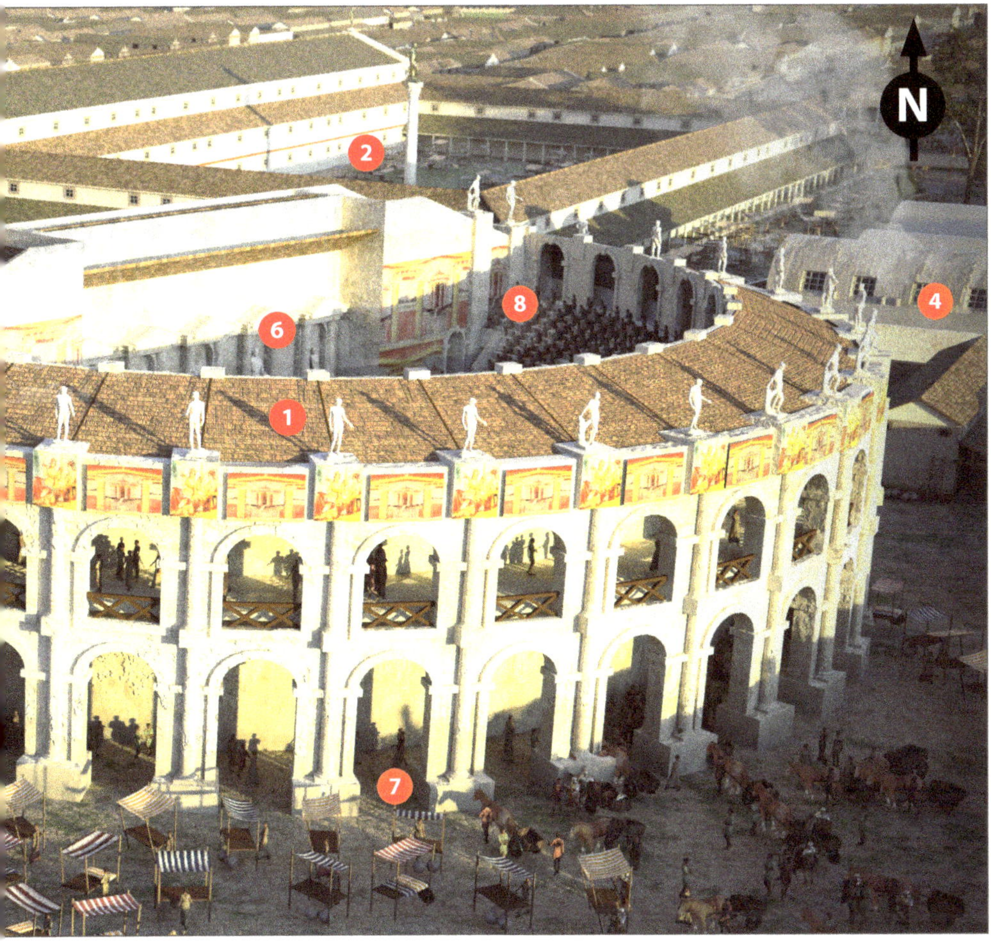

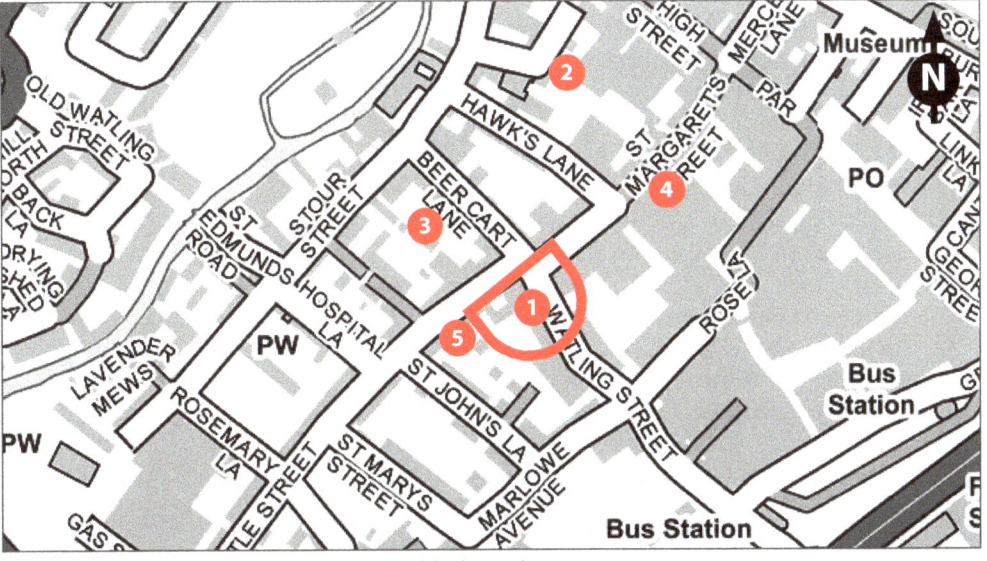

A speculative view of the Basilica and Forum, looking north, 300 CE.

The Basilica and Forum

The *Basilica* and *Forum (public square)* were the most important civic structures in major Roman towns. Although archaeologists are agreed that Canterbury would have had a basilica and forum, little is known about how they looked. The site **may** have been approximately 130m *(426 ft)* long by 85m *(279 ft)* wide. It is also not known exactly when the Basilica and Forum were constructed, but other public buildings were built around 100 CE. Various offices for local administrators and merchants typically surrounded the forum, which often had a colonnade providing shade in summer and shelter in winter. There would also have been market stalls selling food and household items sourced from all over the Roman Empire. Some of the items traded here could have included: Middle-Eastern dried fruit, Spanish seafood and German glassware, all of which have been found in Roman Britain.

Key
- Roman Wall (Basilica)
- ① Basilica
- ② Forum
- ③ Market stalls
- ④ Public Bathhouse

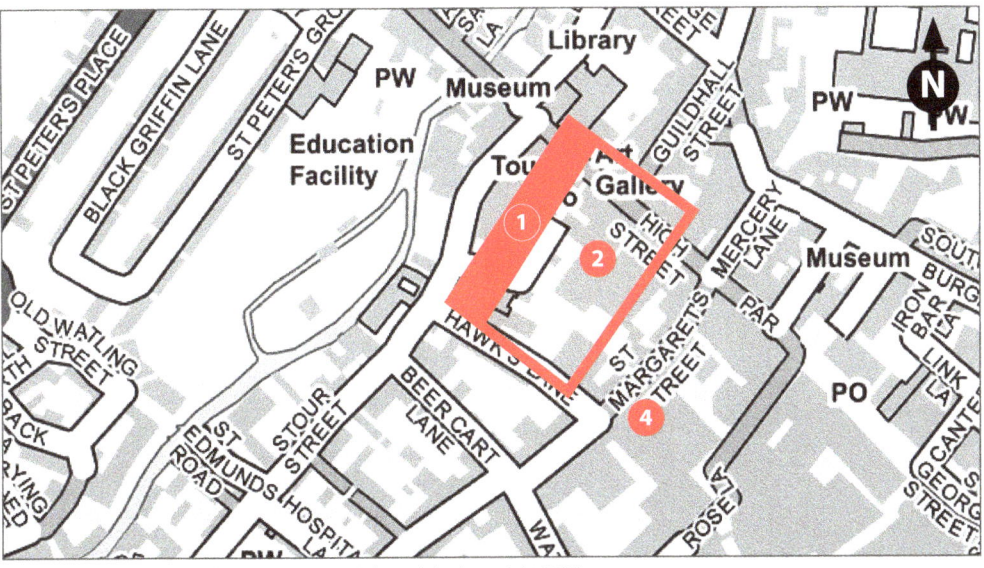

A view of how the Temple Precinct may have looked, looking north, around 300 CE.

The Temple Precinct

Roman Canterbury had several temples within its walls, including one which was surrounded by a massive portico. Currently it is not known exactly what the temple looked like and its exact location. Above is a **speculative** view showing how the temple and its precinct may have looked.

Temples in Roman Britain were mostly dedicated to one of the Romans' many gods such as Jupiter,[1] but it is not known which god this temple was dedicated to.

Archaeologists have found the remains of large columns, hundreds of wall mouldings, veneers and more, some of which came from Italy. Roman temples in Britain typically followed two main designs, one called Romano-Celtic and the other rectangular, which is thought to be the style/design of this temple.

1. Jupiter was the Roman god of the sky and thunder.

Key

1. *Temple*
2. *Temple Precinct Wall*
3. *Basilica*
4. *Roman Theatre*
5. *Triumphal Arch*
6. *West Gate*

 Canterbury Roman Museum has artefacts from the Roman Temple Precinct.

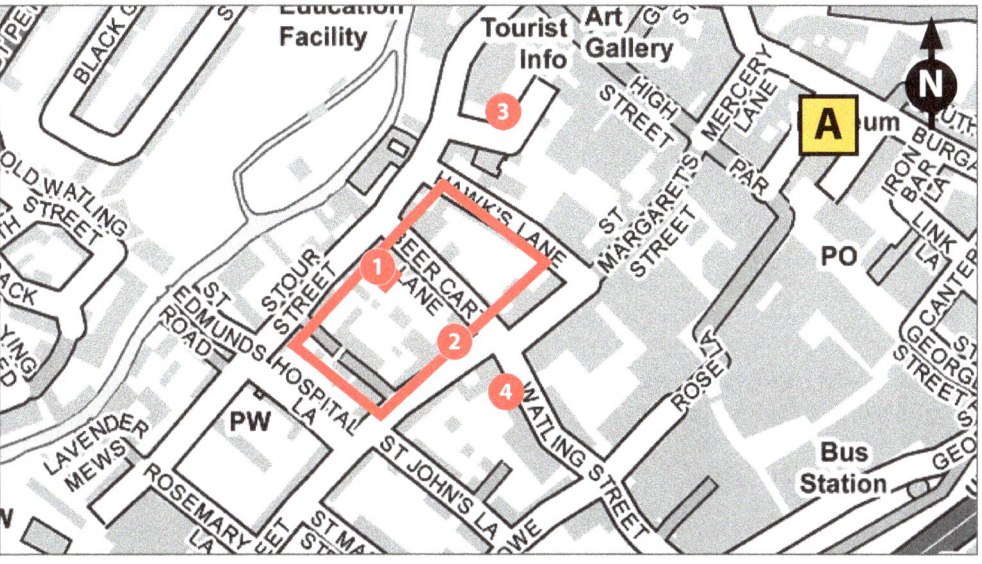

A speculative view of the Public Bathhouse, looking north, 300 CE.

The Public Bathhouse

Most Roman towns had large public bathhouses, where people could bathe and socialise. Evidence for a public bathhouse has been found in the centre of Canterbury, which is believed to have been built around 100 CE. It would have had a *Caldarium (hot room), Tepidarium (warm room)* and a *Frigidarium (cold room)*. The public bathhouse is also thought to have had an indoor swimming pool *(piscina)* and an outside exercise area *(palestra)*. There is also evidence that the site had underfloor heating, which would have been a warm luxury for Canterbury's citizens, especially in the depths of winter, while they washed themselves[1]. The public bathhouse was probably upgraded various times until the end of the Roman period, around 412 CE.

1. *The Romans did not have soap products, so instead used oil and scraped the oil off with a curved implement called a strigil.*

Key

1. Public Bathhouse
2. Tepidarium
3. Caldarium
4. Frigidarium
5. Furnace
6. Piscina
7. Palestra
8. Basilica/Forum
9. Roman Townhouse (see page 20)

A Canterbury Roman Museum. Items from the Public Bathhouse are on display inside the museum.

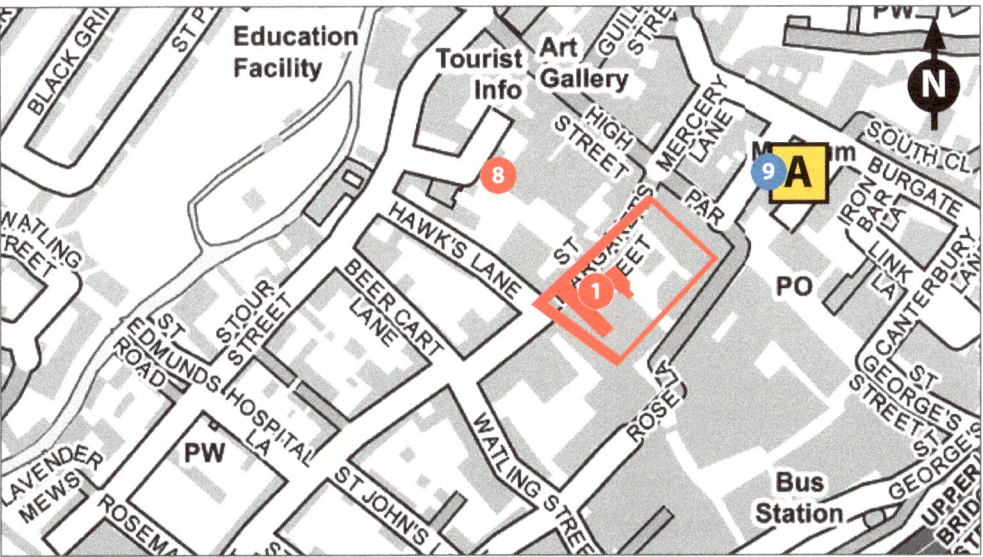

A view of the Townhouse, looking north, around 300 CE.

The Townhouse

In 1868 workmen uncovered a mosaic while constructing a drainage system. It was not until after WW2 that it was discovered to be part of a large Roman townhouse. It is thought to have been built around 90 CE and then extended around 110 CE. Mosaic floors were added around 300 CE, some of which can be seen in the Canterbury Roman Museum, which is built around the townhouse. The townhouse would have been large by today's standards, with a water supply, heated floors and roof tiles. Rooms in the townhouse included: the *Triclinium*[1] *(dining room)*, the *Tablinum (study)*, *Culina (kitchen)* and the *Vestibulum (entrance hall)*. The owners possibly had an ornamental garden, full of flowers, shrubs and ornate statues.

1. Here the owner would have entertained guests, possibly wealthy merchants or politicians.

Key

— Roman Town Wall
1 Townhouse
2 Garden
3 Basilica and Forum

A Canterbury Roman Museum. Sections of the Roman townhouse are on display in the museum.

N
1
2

N
A
1
3
ST PETER'S STREET
ST PETER'S PLACE
TOWER WY
BLACK GRIFFIN LANE
ST PETER'S GROVE
THE FRIARS
ALL SAINTS LA
BEST LA
ORANGE STREET
GUILDHALL STREET
MERCERY LANE
PAR
ST MARGARET'S STREET
HAWK'S LANE
BEER CART LANE
STOUR STREET
ST EDMUNDS ROAD
HOSPITAL LA
WATLING STREET
LAVENDER MEWS
ST JOHN'S
ROSE LA
SOUTH CL
BURGATE
SUN BAR LA
LINK LA
CANTERBURY LANE
BURGATE LANE
ST GEORGE'S STREET
ST GEORGE'S
UPPER BRIDGE STREET
LOWER BRIDGE STREET
MONASTERY STREET
HAVELOCK ST
LOVE LA
IVY LANE
PW
Education Facility
Library
Museum
Tourist Info
Art Gallery
PO
Bus Station

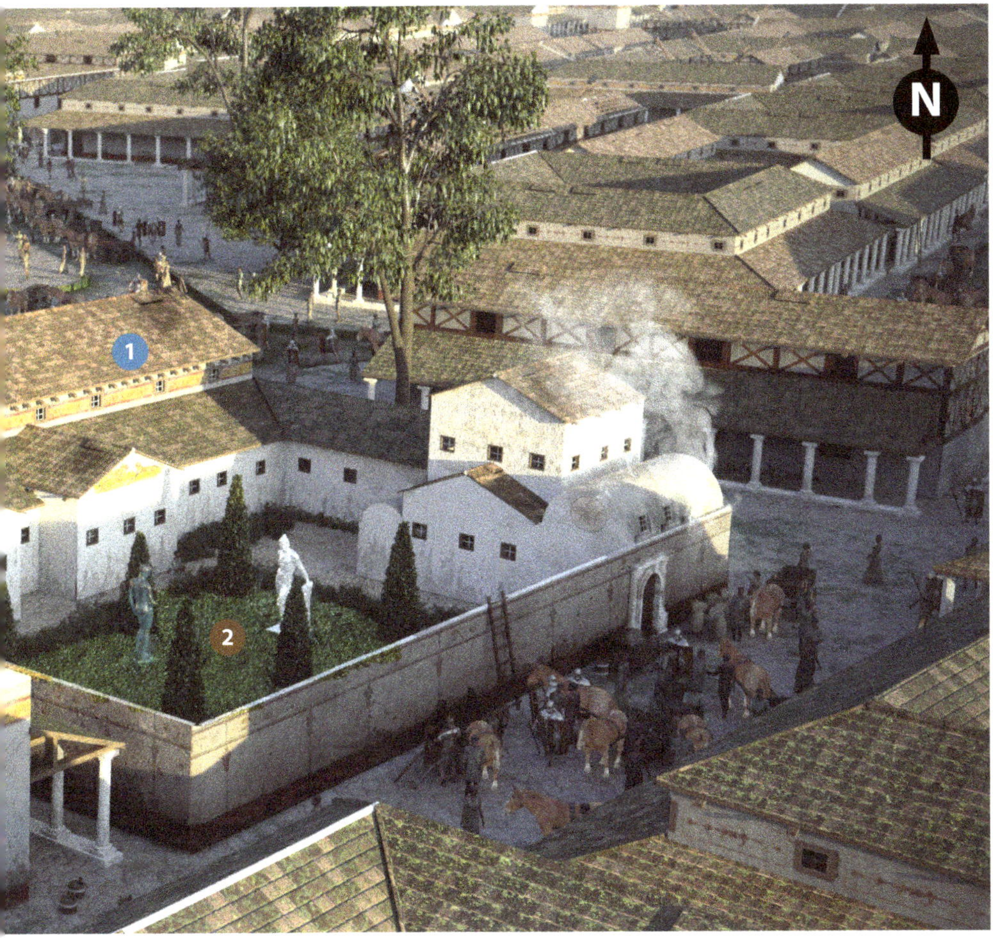

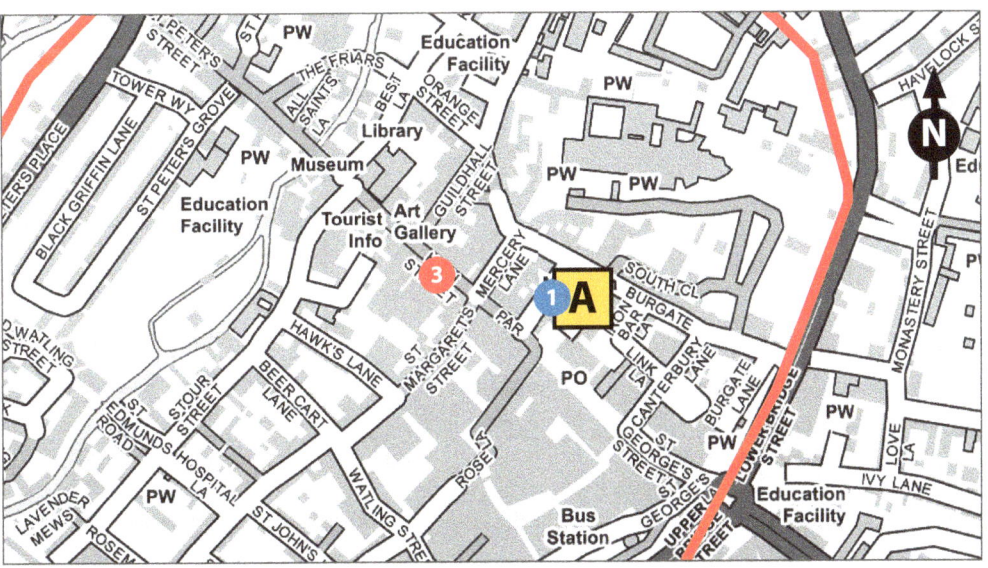

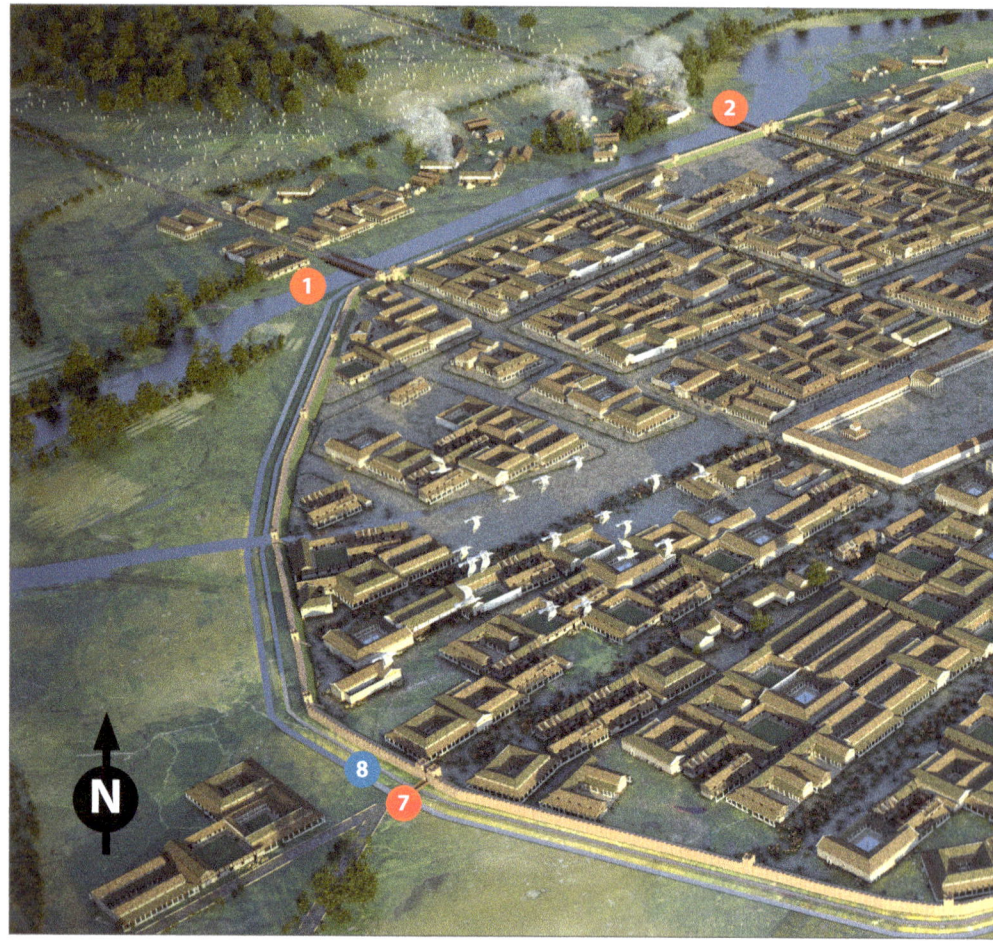

A suggested view of the Roman Town Wall around 300 CE, looking north.

The Roman Town Wall

Most of the Roman Town Wall is no longer visible, but the medieval wall which surrounds large sections of central Canterbury follows the line of the original Roman Town Wall. The wall was built by around 290 CE and was around 2.3m (7.5 ft) thick. Around this time a large defensive system, known as the *'forts of the Saxon Shore'* was being constructed. This stretched from Brancaster in North Norfolk down to Porchester on the south coast and was a response to increasing raids by *Saxon* pirates.[1] Other Roman towns, including London, were also improving their defences, as increasingly the Roman Empire was starting to crumble. Around Canterbury's Roman wall were fortified gatehouses, which defended the roads into Canterbury, including from London. Most of these gatehouses are no longer visible except for a small section of Queningate.

1. The Saxons came from an area around northern Germany.

Key

— Roman Town Wall
1. London Gate
2. West Gate
3. North Gate
4. Queningate[2]
5. Burgate
6. Ridingate
7. Worth Gate
8. Roman Town Wall[2]

2. See online for exact location details, as they are small sections and can be hard to find.

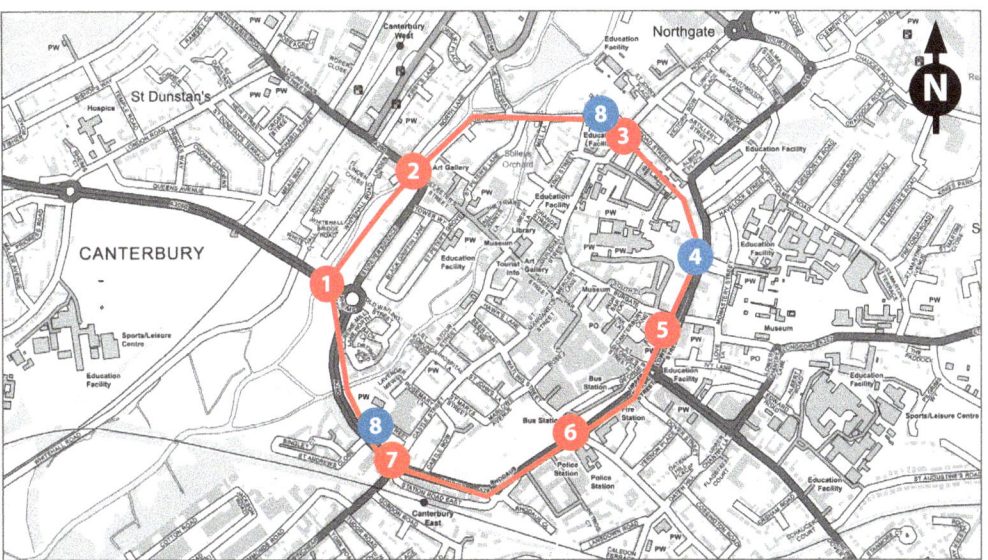

24. Ridingate

A view showing Ridingate around 300 CE, looking north.

Ridingate

Ridingate, located on the south-east section of the Roman Town Wall, connected Canterbury with Dover *(Dubris, as it was known then)*. It is not known what Ridingate was called in Roman times and its exact design had been undecided until a major excavation in 1986. In that excavation part of one of the door mechanisms was uncovered, which is now on display in the Canterbury Roman Museum.

We can imagine that if someone tried to attack the town, deep double ditches would have forced them to attack the gatehouses. The gatehouses themselves acted as funnels, drawing the attackers in under constant defensive fire from stones and spears. If somehow they got through all that, they still had to breach the huge wooden gates and by then Roman reinforcements from other towns would be on the way!

Key

— Roman Wall
1. Ridingate
2. Worth Gate
3. London Gate
4. Burgate
5. Queningate
6. Defensive ditch
7. Watling Street to Dover
A. Canterbury Roman Museum

N
6
7

N
A
1
2
3
4
5
Museum
Education Facility
Tourist Info
Art Gallery
PW
PO
Bus Station
Fire Station
Police Station
Canterbury East
ST PETERS PL
BLACK GRIFFIN
GUILDHALL STREET
HIGH STREET
MERCERY LANE
SOUTH CL
BURGATE
BURGATE LANE
CANTERBURY LANE
LINK LA
ST GEORGE'S STREET
ST GEORGE'S LA
UPPER BRIDGE STREET
LOWER BRIDGE STREET
MONASTERY STREET
LONGPORT A257
LOWER CHANTRY LANE
IVY LANE
LOVE LA
ALBERT ROAD
EDWARD ROAD
DOVER STREET
VERNON PLACE
OATEN HILL PLACE
OATEN HILL
UPPER CHANTRY LA
FLAGSTAFF COURT
COSSINGTON
ERSHAM ROAD
HAWK'S LANE
ST MARGARET'S STREET
BEER CART LANE
STOUR STREET
ST EDMUNDS ROAD
HOSPITAL LA
ST JOHN'S LA
WATLING STREET
ROSE LA
MARLOWE AVENUE
ST MARYS STREET
CASTLE STREET
ROSEMARY LA
LAVENDER MEWS
GAS STREET
CASTLE ROW
OLD WATLING STREET
NORTH LANE
CREINE MILL LANE
BACK LA
DRIVING SHED
RHEIMS WAY
A290
ANDREWS CLOSE
PIN HILL
RHODAUS
A28
STATION ROAD EAST
GORDON ROAD
TUDOR
RHODAUS CL
PETROS CT

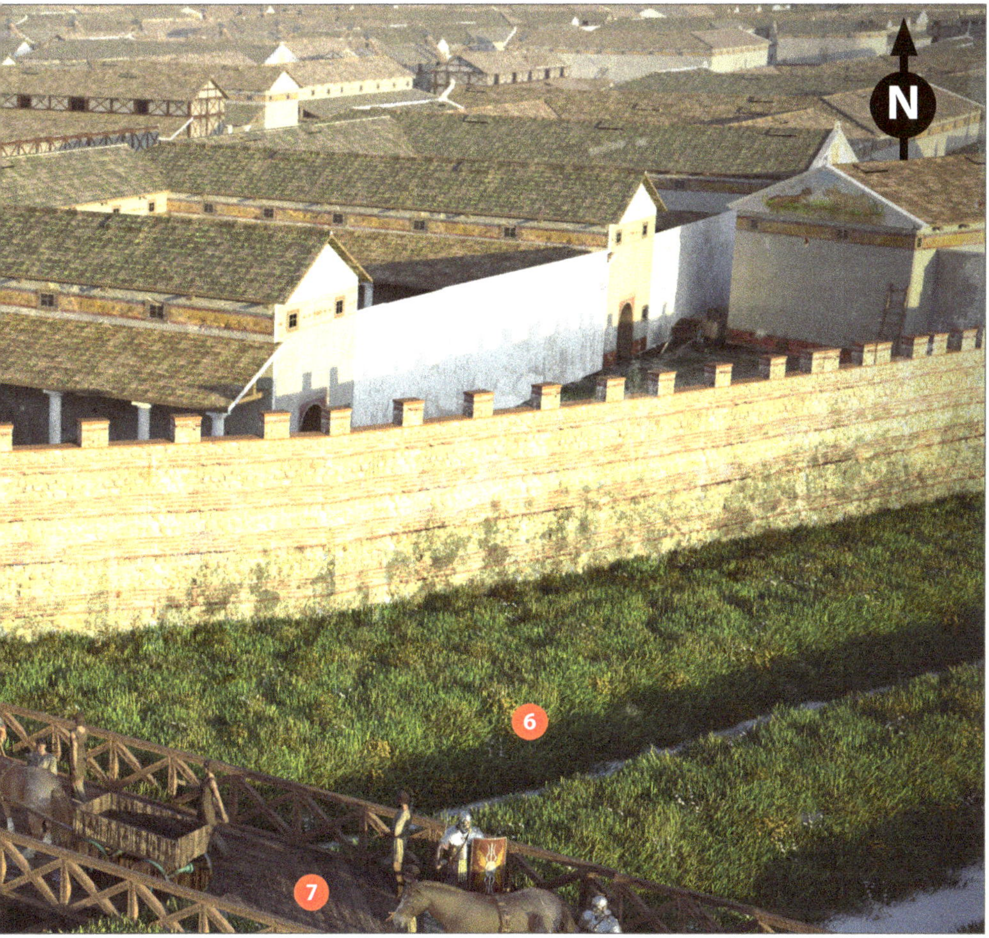

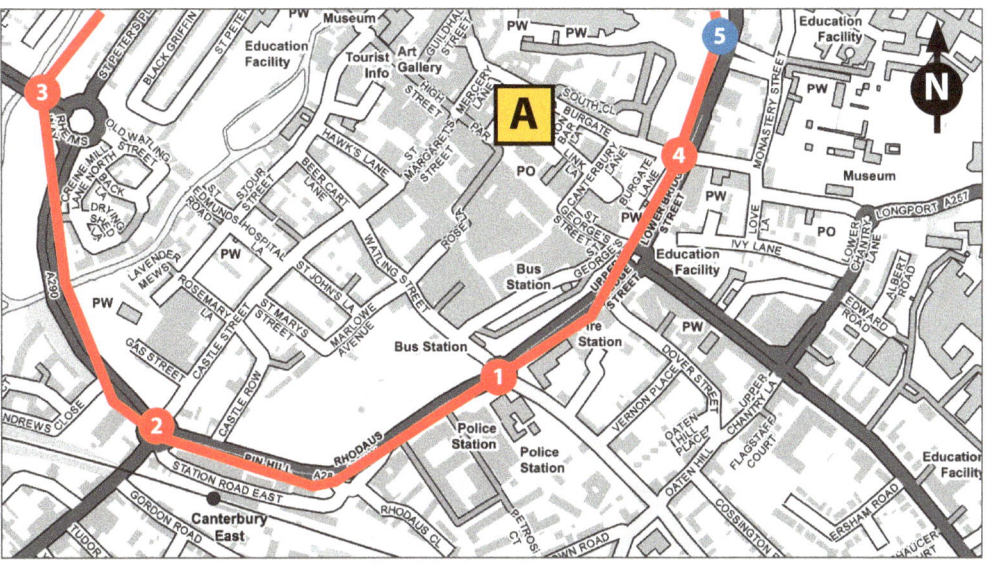

A view showing typical weapons and equipment used by the Legio II Augusta.

The Roman Army

During the invasion of 43 CE the Emperor Claudius brought with him four legions, each made up of approximately 5,000 soldiers. The map on the right shows what is thought to have been the original route of the invasion, which would have passed through the area which is now Canterbury.

The image above shows typical equipment used by *Legio II Augusta (Second Legion 'Augustus')*, one of the four legions deployed during the invasion of 43 CE. The *Legio II Augusta* operated mostly in the south of Britain, first establishing roads and fortresses in the south-east area, before moving towards the south-west and the area which is now Wales. The standard soldier was the *Legionary*, organised into a *century* which had 80 soldiers and was commanded by a *Centurion*. *Centuries* were grouped into cohorts, made up of six *centuries*. The entire legion was made up of 10 cohorts and other specialised troops such as auxiliaries.

Key

1. *Pilum (Javelin)*
2. *Scutum (Shield)*
3. *Focale (Scarf)*
4. *Gladius (Sword)*
5. *Galea (Helmet)*
6. *Lorica Segmentata (Body Armour)*
7. *Tunica (Tunic)*
8. *Caligae (Sandals)*

Artefacts from the Roman Army can be seen at the Canterbury Roman Museum.

A possible route used by the Roman Army during the invasion of 43 CE

A *Boulogne*
B *Richborough*
C *Canterbury*
D *Colchester*

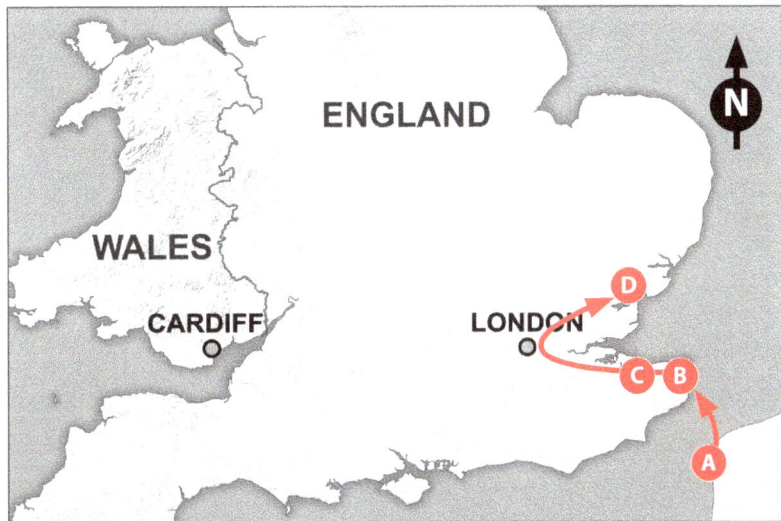

Contains Ordnance Survey data © Crown copyright and database right 2025

*A possible view of the Roman Pottery Kilns, looking **east**, 300 CE.*

The Roman Pottery Kilns

Before the Roman invasion, the buildings in Britain, including Canterbury, were mainly constructed from wattle and daub,[1] with thatch roofs. The Romans brought with them new building materials made from kiln-fired bricks and tiles. Archaeologists have found evidence of kilns which were used by the Romans in Canterbury to manufacture building materials. The main illustration is based on experimental reconstructions, where archaeologists attempted to build Roman kilns and then used them to produce kiln-fired products. As well as building materials, such as tiles and bricks, other items such as pots were also produced locally. These were cheaper versions of others produced across the Roman Empire. There would have been stores for clay, manufacturing areas and stock ready to be delivered in and around Canterbury.

1. A mesh of wooden strips covered with wet clay.

Key

- Roman Walls
- 1 Tile Kiln
- 2 Pottery Kiln
- 3 Cemetery
- 4 Speculative Kiln
- 5 Road towards Whitstable
- 6 Basilica
- 7 Roman Wall

 Canterbury Roman Museum. Roman kiln-fired artefacts can be seen inside the museum.

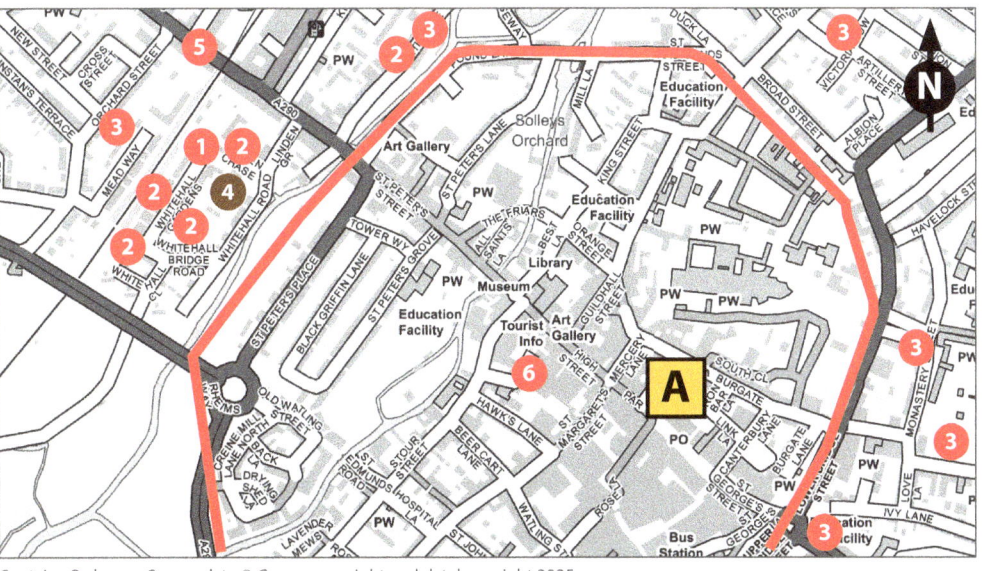

*A speculative view of the Pudding Pan Pots shipwreck site, looking **south**, 180 CE.*

The Pudding Pan Pots

Around 180 CE two Roman ships bound for London were hit by a storm which is thought to have caused them to sink a few miles off present day Herne Bay. They were carrying Samian ware pottery produced in central Gaul.[1]

As the ships broke up, their cargo was strewn across the shallow sandbanks and the ships' location was lost in the silty water. But over 1,600 years later fishing boats started to record finding brown shiny pots in excellent condition from the sea-floor. The pots were treasured by people that found them and they were used to make a special pudding, which is where the area got its name: Pudding Pan Rock.

On the bottom of the pots were stamps showing the names of the potters who made them. At least 285 pots have been recorded and some have been taken by their owners as far away as Australia.

1. Lezoux, central France.

Key

1. *Possible shipwreck site*
2. *Present day town of Herne Bay*
3. *Canterbury*
4. *London*
5. *Samian ware pottery*
6. *North Sea*
7. *Sailors, to scale*

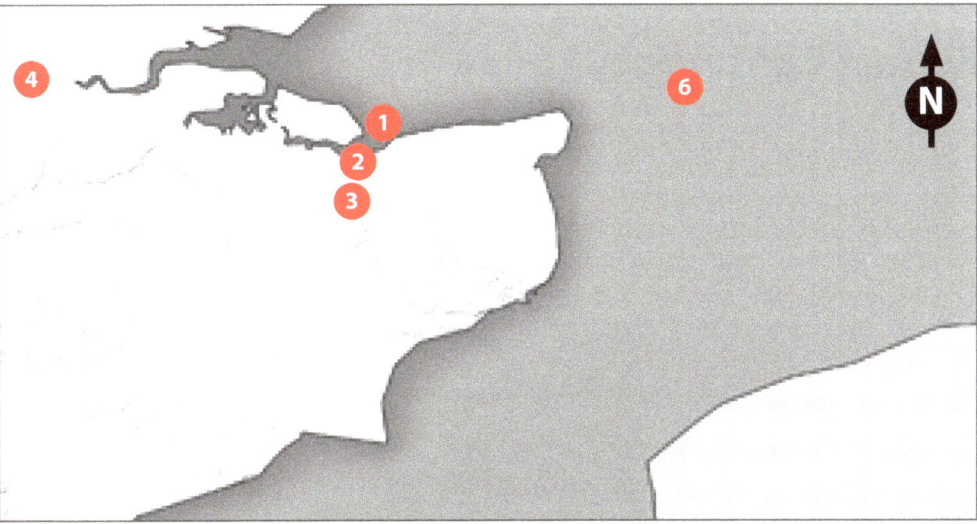

The approximate location of the Roman ships, wrecked near Canterbury

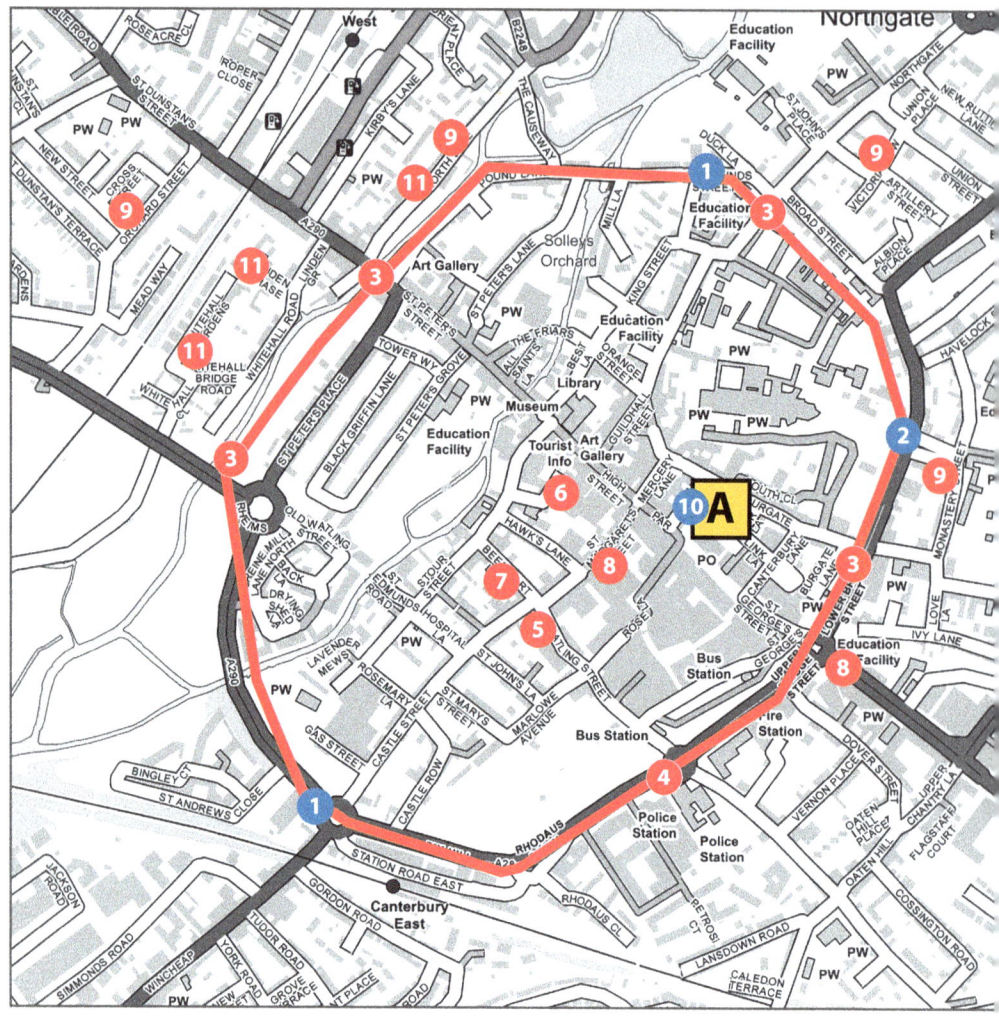

Roman Canterbury today

Most of Roman Canterbury is now no longer visible, except for a couple of small sections of the Roman Wall.
The Canterbury Roman Museum has an extensive range of Roman mosaics, artefacts and displays. The sites shown on this map are also explored in more detail in the main part of this book. Unless specified otherwise, the exterior images of Roman Canterbury face north, so that you can compare the past with the present day maps. Check online for the exact locations of the surviving sections of the Roman Town Wall and Queningate as they are quite small and hard to find.

Key

1 *All Blue circles show a Roman site, which has visible remains*

2 *All Red circles show a Roman site, which has no visible remains*

— *All Red lines show a Roman wall, which has no visible remains*

A *The Yellow square shows a museum, which has visible Roman artefacts/remains*

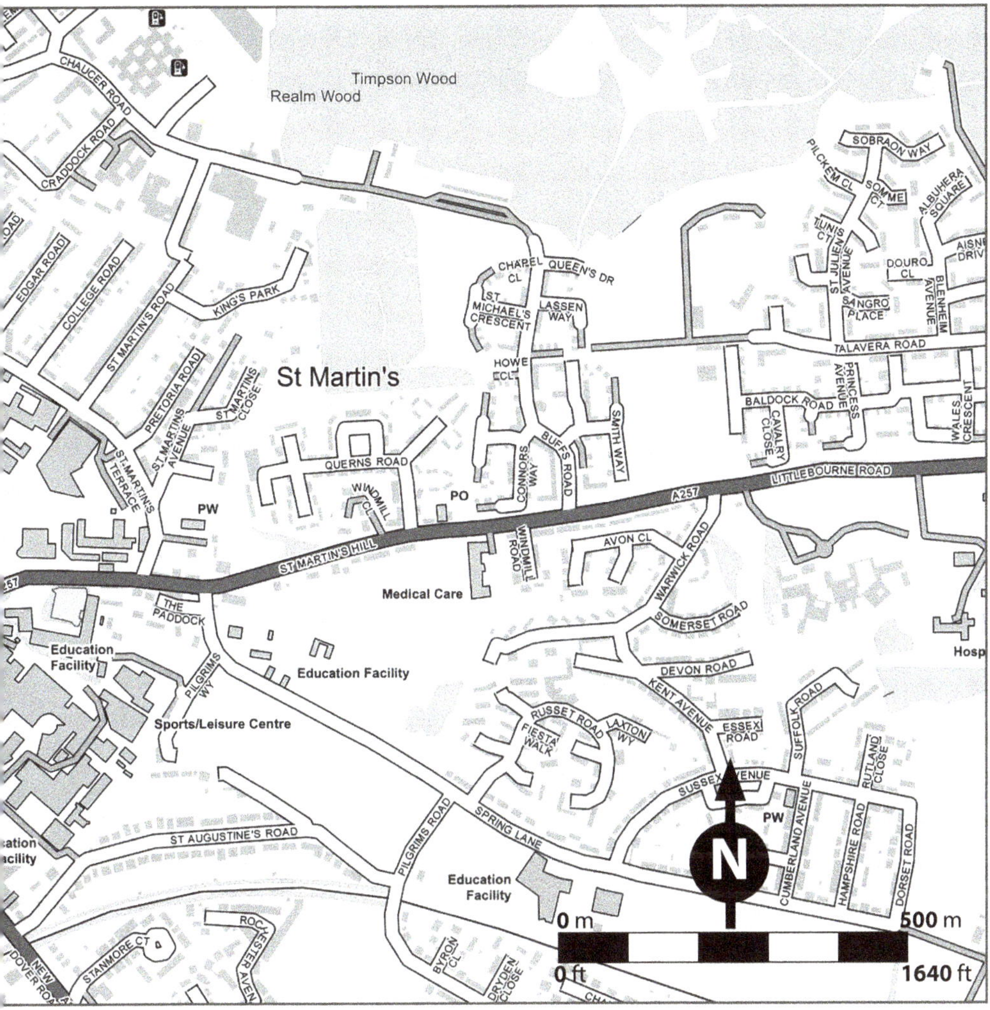

Contains Ordnance Survey data © Crown copyright and database right 2025

— Roman Wall (p 22)
1. Roman Wall (p. 22)
2. Queningate (p. 22)
3. Roman Gatehouse (p. 22)
4. Ridingate (p. 22/24)
5. Roman Theatre (p.12)
6. Basilica/Forum (p. 14)
7. Temple Precinct (p. 16)
8. Public Bathhouse (p.18)
9. Roman Cemetery (p. 10)
10. Roman Townhouse (p. 20)
11. Roman Kilns (p. 28)

A Canterbury Roman Museum.
The museum has extensive displays, artefacts and mosaics from the Roman period, including artefacts from the Roman Army (page 26) and the Pudding Pan Pots (page 30).

First published Jan 2025
ISBN 978-1-0683525-0-8 *(Paperback)*
First Edition

Designed and published by JC3DVIS. www.jc3dvis.co.uk
Book design © 2025 Joseph Chittenden

All the images in this guide were produced by JC3DVIS.
Contains Ordnance Survey data © Crown copyright and database right 2025

The moral right of the copyright holder has been asserted.

All rights reserved. No part of this publication may be reproduced, distributed or transmitted in any form or by any means, including photocopying, recording, or other electronic or mechanical methods, without the prior written permission of the publisher.

With special thanks to:
Jane Chittenden
Gary Jephcote: Canterbury Roman Museum

Legal disclaimer
Neither the author nor the publisher shall be held liable or responsible to any person or entity with respect to any loss or incidental or consequential damages caused, or alleged to have been caused, directly or indirectly, by the information contained herein.

Bibliography and sources
- KAS: *Canterbury Kiln Site A Roman Pottery Kiln at Canterbury Webster_1.pdf*
- Canterbury Archaeological Trust: *Roman and Anglo Saxon Canterbury Reconstructed*
- Canterbury Archaeological Trust: *Roman Canterbury*
- Canterbury Archaeological Trust: *The Centre of Roman Canterbury c.AD 300*
- *https://peterborougharchaeology.org/the-roman-kiln/*
- *https://webapps.kent.gov.uk/KCC.ExploringKentsPast.Web.Sites.Public/SingleResult.aspx?uid=MKE24922 (Townhouse-under Roman Canterbury Museum)*
- *https://webapps.kent.gov.uk/KCC.ExploringKentsPast.Web.Sites.Public/SingleResult.aspx?uid=MKE4812 (Roman Canterbury)*
- *https://webapps.kent.gov.uk/KCC.ExploringKentsPast.Web.Sites.Public/SingleResult.aspx?uid=MKE4926 (Roman walls)*
- *https://webapps.kent.gov.uk/KCC.ExploringKentsPast.Web.Sites.Public/SingleResult.aspx?uid=MKE5079 (Public Bathhouse)*
- *https://webapps.kent.gov.uk/KCC.ExploringKentsPast.Web.Sites.Public/SingleResult.aspx?uid=MKE92593 (Basilica)*
- *https://webapps.kent.gov.uk/KCC.ExploringKentsPast.Web.Sites.Public/SingleResult.aspx?uid=%27mke10096%27 (Pudding Pan Rock)*
- *https://www.canterburytrust.co.uk/20-centuries*
- Lyle, Marjorie: *Canterbury: 2000 Years of History (Canterbury after the Romans)*
- *Site visit to the Canterbury Roman Museum*
- KAS: *The Topography of Roman Canterbury A Brief Reassessment* (accessed online)
- *https://canterburymuseums.co.uk/canterbury-roman-museum/about-the-roman-museum/*